YOU ARE HERE

YOU ARE HERE

Steffany Barton

Columbus, Ohio

You Are Here

Published by Gatekeeper Press
2167 Stringtown Rd, Suite 109
Columbus, OH 43123-2989
www.GatekeeperPress.com

Copyright © 2020 by Steffany Barton
All rights reserved. Neither this book, nor any parts within it may be sold or reproduced in any form or by any electronic or mechanical means, including information storage and retrieval systems without permission in writing from the author. The only exception is by a reviewer, who may quote short excerpts in a review.

The cover design, interior formatting, typesetting, and editorial work for this book are entirely the product of the author. Gatekeeper Press did not participate in and is not responsible for any aspect of these elements.

ISBN (paperback): 9781662902024

Cover Art by Heather

www.studiothirdeye.com

Color Illustrations by Emily Johnson

www.emilyjohnsonart.com

Black and White Images by

ZDezign

Author Photo by Kelly Daniels

www.thekellygallery.com

Editing by Sara Fae Kosteva

www.thefaegroup.com

This book is dedicated to my dear friends Jim and Cindy. Though we are miles apart, you always manage to bring a smile to my heart.

Author's Note

Blue.

Looking through the windshield as I headed southbound to the grocery store, I was struck, almost breathtaken, by the magnificence of the bluest of blue skies. The soft, splendid, vibrant blueness filled my eyes and lifted my spirits. No jet trails, no smoke puffs, not even a cloud could be seen in the endlessly perfect blue sky. I caught my breath, and I sensed that our beautiful Earth was catching her breath, too. Free from pollution, released from smog, I imagined Earth heaving a sigh of relief.

Blue.

An instant later I began to feel the darkest of blues swallow my heart as I remembered speaking with a wonderful woman the day before. She had worked as a stewardess for nearly two decades and, with commercial flights grounded, she had been furloughed from her job. She prayed her unemployment would come in before her savings ran out; though she wanted to work, she could not. Her means of well-being seemed very much out of her hands.

Maybe the Earth could breathe, but in that moment, I remembered sensing this woman's anxiety. She most certainly could not.

Blue.

Baby blue eyes wide open, my beautiful daughter, next to me in the passenger's seat, carefully looped the elastic band of her face mask around her left ear.

"The world is so different," she began. Then, muffled as the mask covered her mouth, "I don't think it will ever be the same." She looked at me, sweet and tender. I smiled at her, struggling to keep tears back, "I know, love. I know. This is such a unique time. But I'm glad we're together."

The rest of that afternoon I felt hopeful then helpless, happy then sad, peppy then drained, and worn out to numb. Why do some win so that some can lose? Why do some have to die and some get to live? Why do some prosper while others scarcely scrape by. Why?

I arrived home from the grocery run shortly before dinner and went through the motions to prepare our food. Preoccupied with the pandemic, I barely touched my meal.

After clean up, I decided to write for a few minutes, hoping a bit of creativity would help me get back to the truth I know. Yes, challenges can rock us to the core and distractions will knock us off course, and I could feel myself slipping. Yet, the soul of me, the true nature of me understood then, as I know now, that somehow, in wonderful and miraculous ways, we will get through this.

Words started flowing, and I noticed I was writing a poem. More words tumbled from my pen, and I discovered this was more than a poem, it was a proclamation, an invitation to remember what has always been true.

Yes, we are in the midst of a global pandemic. Sometimes though, we go through personal pandemics. The loss of a job, a change in relationship, an unexpected financial hardship, the death of a loved one are challenges that can prompt us to lockdown joy, furlough happiness, distance from our support. We've all had times where we hunker down just to survive.

The river of life can be wild and raging, ravaging our emotional landscape, stripping our resources, leaving us vulnerable and raw. When what was ceases to exist, we may grapple with a sense of hope for what might be.

How can we let go *and* hold on?

As I continued to write, I felt this river of life coursing through me, shouting, roiling, tumbling recklessly. Yet, verse after verse, the sounds of the current began to change and the feelings in me shifted. As I listened, I heard something soft and profound.

Every moment is a gift. We can ignore the gift and leave it untouched. We can reject it, because maybe we've been given gag gifts or nasty-grams before. We can throw it away because we've been taught that the world is disposable. We can shrug it off and forget the magic, we can give our gift away hoping to please someone else.

Or, we can open the gift, the present.

You are here.

I believe Here is the intersection where your self meets your Self. Here is the moment when you decide to show up and live. Here is the instant you become aware that you have a body AND a spirit. Here is the miracle of remembering that you take on roles, but you are a full, complete, amazing soul. Here is choosing to release the need to control. Here is where you glimpse light around you and see light *inside* you.

Here is seeing, hearing, feeling, and knowing not with your ordinary senses, but with the extraordinary love in your heart.

Here is more than just now. Here is *you* in the now.

You are here.

Please, don't start reading this book just yet. Take a moment to hold it. Put the book up to your heart and feel it. Flip through the pages and touch the cover. Then as you begin, dip into the pictures and slip into the spaces between the words. Take this book in, sit with it, slowly savor the goodness. Experience this book, because it's more than just sentences.

This is a journey through the past and beyond the reaches of time.

Welcome. I am glad you're here.

With love,

Steff

You are here.
The world seems new
And uncertain, unknown.
What should you do?

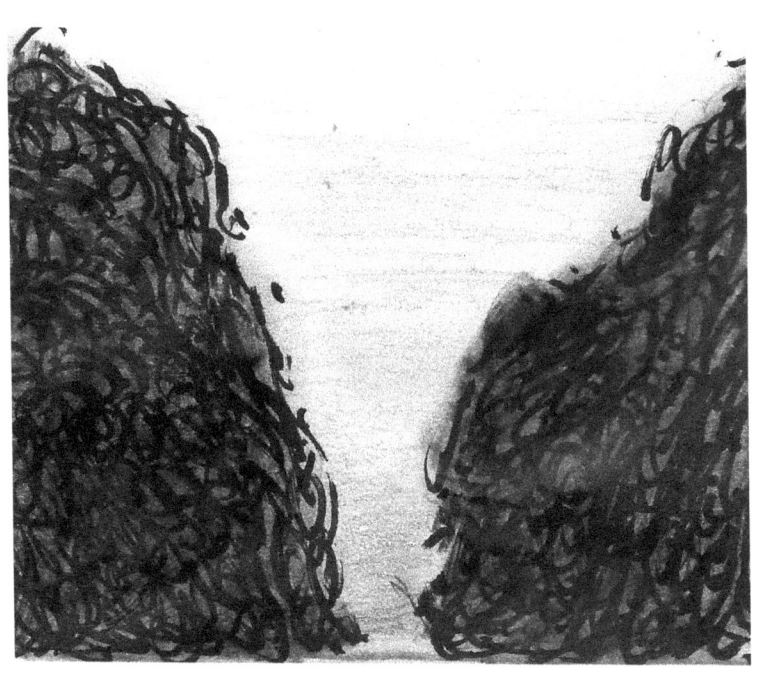

The old patterns and habits,
The paths tried and true,
Are rickety and rocky.
What can you do?

Maybe you were fine,
Or happy enough.
You certainly didn't want to
Deal with this stuff.

Who wants to change?
Routine is quite easy.
Rock the boat too much
And you're bound to get queasy.

But suddenly one day
The world crashed down,
Uncertainty looming,
No answers found.

Perhaps this will work.
Oh, wait! It won't.
Here, try this—
Oh, stop! Please don't.

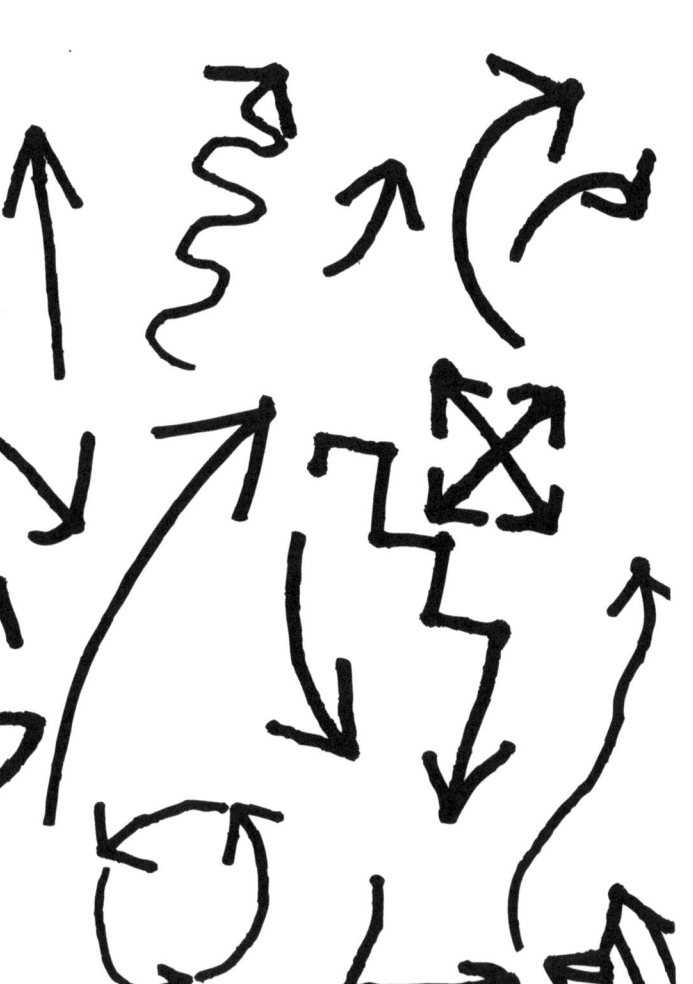

Hunkered at home,
You had to stay put,
Striving to stay steady
With constant change afoot.

Tightly you bunkered,
Afraid to move.
It's hard to feel grounded
When you've lost your groove.

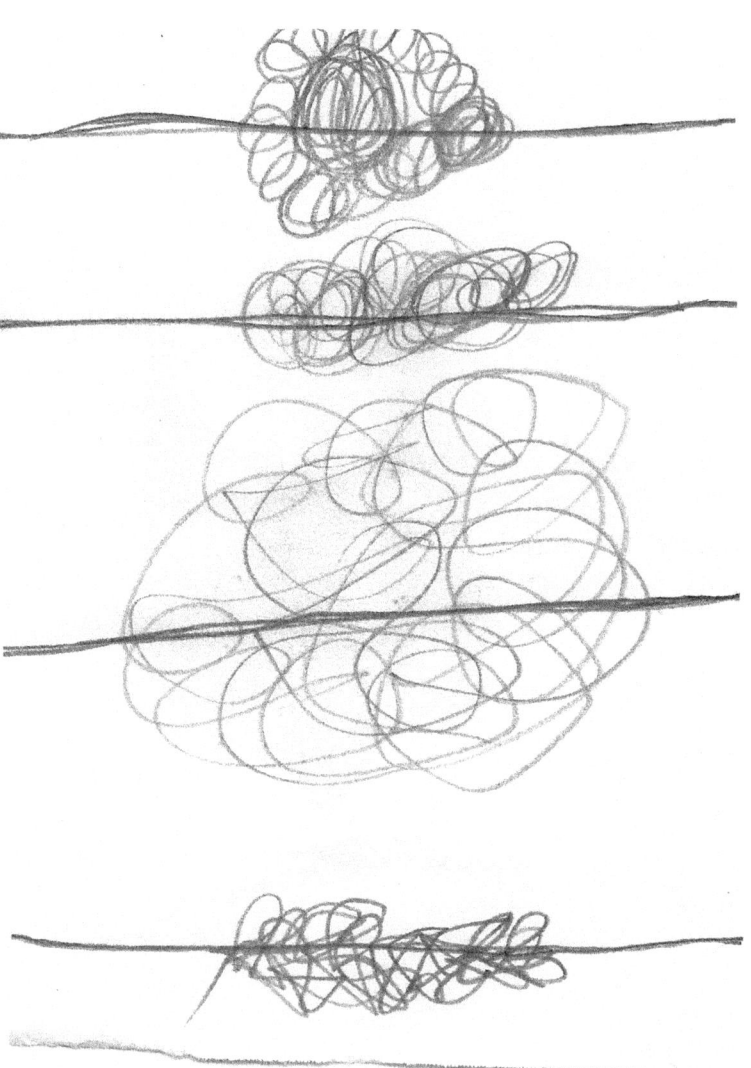

Yet slowly and surely
The storm started to clear.
The worst was behind you,
Bright skies drew near.

Alas,
Unused parts get
Rusty and stiff.
"You can come out now," they say.
But you think: "What if ... ?"

What if you dive right in,
Sink or swim,
Go out on a limb,
Just to start over again?

What if it's too soon,
Or maybe you're too late.
Perhaps it's just no use;
Give up and accept your fate.

Or maybe,

Just maybe,

This change was a gift.

Maybe,

Just maybe,

You feel a small shift:

A spark, a light,
A thought clear and true.
Maybe you'll pave a way
That's perfect for YOU.

You don't have to go back
To what's always been.
You can choose to be different
With a change from within.

From mild to wild
Or meek to sleek,
From doubtful to hopeful
With courage in heaps.

Ready to say "Yes!"
Or happy saying "No."
You can choose how to live
When you trust what you know.

Know you are wonderful,
Know you are wise.
Know when you smile,
Light shines in your eyes.

Know you are here
Filled with grace;
Know that your life
Is a sacred space
For Love.

You've made it this far.
You've seen it through.
Keep going, my friend,
A new day awaits you.

Today you could take a chance,
Or learn to dance.
You could boldly speak
About your stance
On the oceans, the forests,
The rivers, the trees,
Animals, the homeless,
The poor, the elderly.

You might just decide,
Shocking but true,
That expectations of others
Will no longer limit you.
Whew!

You could read a book,
Or pen one yourself.
Visit the library.
See your work on the shelf.

You could create an altar:
A sweet little nook,
Judgment-free,
Where you can look
In your heart.

You could take a nap,
Or spend the day
Just watching the clouds.
It's okay
To slow down and
Breathe ...

You could
Accept who you are,
Celebrate your soul,
Appreciate the past,
And then choose to let go
Of the guilt, the self-doubt,
The "ifs," "ands," or "buts."
Hanging on to that stuff
Will make you go nuts.

You might plant a seed
Or a single flower
Because you now accept
The incredible power of one:
YOU.

You've made it this far,
You've seen it through.
This day is a gift
And so, friend, are YOU.

You are here.